KU-244-476

Heather Brown

CONTENTS

INTRODUCTION

Gymnastics is a fun and dynamic sport for everyone. It's a great way to stay fit and healthy and to learn new skills. You can also make good friends at your club and you will have the opportunity to travel and perform in competitions together.

HISTORY OF GYMNASTICS

Gymnastics is one of the oldest Olympic sports. It was included in the first modern Olympic Games, held in Athens in 1896. On that occasion, 285 athletes – all of them men – competed in the Games. Women gymnasts first competed in the Olympics at the 1928 Games, held in Amsterdam. The high levels of artistry and technical skill in gymnastics make it a popular spectator sport around the world.

GUIDE TO ARROWS

Throughout the book we have used red arrows like this ➡ to indicate the action and direction of the body.

EQUIPMENT

I n artistic gymnastics, women compete in four events: vault, asymmetric bars, beam and the floor. Men compete in six events: floor, vault, pommel horse, rings, parallel bars and the high bar.

VAULT

Gymnasts run down a runway that is padded or carpeted and hurdle onto the springboard. They then spring onto the vault with their hands and push off into the air before landing on a safety mat on the other side. While in the air gymnasts might perform moves, such as twists and somersaults, before landing (see pages 10-13).

Springboard

All the pieces of apparatus are arranged in the gym so that gymnasts can use them safely.

FLOOR

The floor area is made of wooden panels mounted on springs (known as a sprung floor) and covered in carpet. The sprung floor enables gymnasts to perform high-tumbling sequences. Floor routines feature acrobatics, leaps, jumps, pirouettes and dance (see pages 14-17). The edge of the floor area is marked with a line and you lose points if you step outside this area.

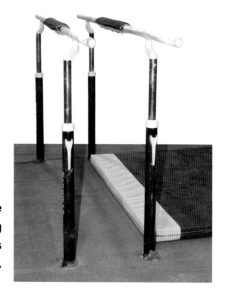

PARALLEL BARS

Consisting of rails made of fibreglass, the parallel bars are set at the same height and are the same length. Male gymnasts perform swinging movements which allow them to rotate above and below the bars (see pages 18-21).

The rings hang 2.75 metres above the floor from cables that are attached to the ceiling. The rings are 50 centimetres apart and gymnasts must perform a routine involving swinging and strength movements (see pages 22-25).

Also known as the 'uneven bars', the asymmetric bars consist of two fibreglass bars set at different heights. A springboard can be used to mount the apparatus. In competition, a routine on the asymmetric bars must be continuous, without any stops or adjustments (see pages 26-29).

Springboard

When practising, gymnasts use thick safety mats to land on. These are soft and will break their fall.

The pommel horse has two handles (or pommels) attached to it and two legs that are attached to the floor. Gymnasts perform a routine of movements including, scissors and circles using the whole length of the horse (see pages 30-33).

Gymnasts tumble and dance along a balance beam that is perched above the floor. The maximum allowed time for the beam exercise is 1 minute and 30 seconds (see pages 34-37).

Selection of beams for different levels of gymnasts.

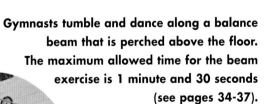

The high bar is a single bar standing 2.75 metres high. Gymnasts perform 'release and catch' movements high above the bar, and dismount with multiple somersaults or twists (see pages 38-41).

WHAT TO WEAR & TRAINING

In competition, women gymnasts wear leotards. These can be long sleeved or short sleeved. Male gymnasts generally wear a leotard piece with shorts, but for the pommel horse, parallel bars, rings and high bar, they wear 'whites'. These are a pair of white or coloured trousers which attach at the ankles. Whites allow the judges to see a gymnast's body line when he completes his routines.

Leotards

Shorts

Coloured whites

FOOTWEAR

Many gymnasts prefer to work barefoot, however special footwear is permitted in competition for both men and women gymnasts. Gymnastics shoes should be in good condition, have non-slip soles and fit well. Gymnasts should never wear jewellery, in training or in competition, as it may result in an accident or damage to the apparatus. Long hair should be tied back to avoid distraction.

HANDGUARDS

When performing on the asymmetric bars many gymnasts wear handguards or grips. These protect the hands from injuries, such as blisters. Traditional grips are made from a variety of materials, such as leather or suede.

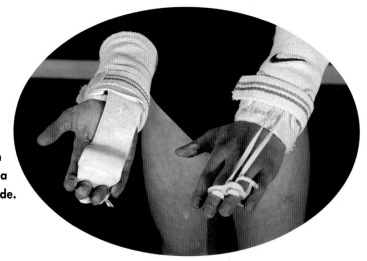

Leotards

Whites

Elite gymnasts preparing for World Championships and the Olympic Games can train for as many as 30 hours per week. It takes sheer hard work, commitment, a love of the sport and natural talent to become a world gymnastics champion. Hours of practice are needed to reach the top in gymnastics, and as elite gymnasts progress, so too does the time they need to invest in training.

PARENTAL SUPPORT

This tough training regime requires support from parents and from schools, as gymnasts need a flexible study timetable to allow them to train during the day and to travel to competitions.

PHYSICAL PREPARATION

To advance in gymnastics, you must prepare your body physically by doing strength and flexibility exercises. Your coach should prepare a strength programme for you that suits your age and physical development, addresses your areas of weakness and states the type of strength required for improvement.

Flexibility is very important too. Flexibility is the range of movement in a joint. It allows you to perform skills correctly, safely and with grace.

CHALK

Using magnesium carbonate or chalk will help you keep your grip and prevent you from slipping when performing on the asymmetric bars. It absorbs perspiration and allows you to keep contact with the bars. It helps to prevent blisters, as it reduces friction between the bars and your hands.

WARMING UP & STRETCHING

You must warm-up before you undertake any form of physical activity. Warming up prepares your body for exercise as it increases the blood flow to your muscles and provides them with added oxygen. The warm-up will also mentally prepare you for your training session ahead and reduce the chance of injury. Once you have warmed up by running or jogging around your gym, you should do some stretching exercises.

THIGH STRETCH

Lift one foot behind you and hold it in your hand. Your standing foot should be flat. Hold the position for 10 seconds and repeat with the other leg. You will feel the stretch in your thigh muscle.

SHOULDER STRETCH

Hold one arm straight out in front of you. Move it across your body and apply pressure with the inside of your elbow of the other arm. Hold the stretch for 10 seconds and repeat with the other arm.

BRIDGE

Start lying on your back with your knees bent and your hands on the floor by the side of your head. Push through your shoulders to extend your back into an arch shape. To exit out of the bridge gently bend your knees and your elbows and lower your body to the ground. This is a good exercise to warm up your back.

Keep your legs and arms as straight as possible.

ROCKING

Sit with your knees bent, hug them and place your hands on both shins. Lift your feet and point your toes. Gently rock backwards and forwards. You should do this after you have done a bridge, as it allows your back muscles to relax.

TOP TIP
It is important to stretch your muscles gently. If you force your stretching, you may injure yourself.

Left leg splits

THE SPLITS

By practising the splits, you will increase the flexibility in your hips and hamstrings. There are three positions in which the splits can be performed; with the right leg in front, the left leg in front and with your legs out to each side (called the box splits).

STRADDLE STRETCH

The straddle position is where your legs are spread wide in front of you. Sit up straight in the straddle position. Your legs should be straight and toes pointed. Reach out with your arms to the side.

JAPANA

Sit in the straddle position with your knees facing towards the ceiling and your toes pointed. Aim to lie your tummy flat on the floor in front of you.

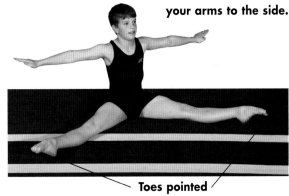

Toes pointed

THE SWIM THROUGH

This technique will stretch your inner thigh muscles, try and relax into the stretch and hold for 10 seconds.

STEP 1

Sit in the straddle position. Then stretch forward and lie your tummy flat on the floor in front of you. Stretch your legs back into the box splits position.

STEP 2

Bring your legs together and finish lying on your tummy in a straight position.

Box splits position.

Finish position for the swim through.

TOP TIP
Wear your tracksuit during warm-up sessions to prevent your body temperature from dropping.

VAULT

Vaulting is fast and dynamic. Gymnasts run at high speed along a runway, jump onto the springboard, reach for the vaulting table and propel themselves high into the air, landing safely on the other side of the apparatus.

THE HURDLE STEP

To practise your hurdle step technique, take off from the springboard and do a straight jump onto a safety mat. Repeat this exercise until you gain confidence, then move on to the vault runway.

Lean forward into the run.

STEP 1

Run up to the springboard with speed and determination. Lean forward into the run with your head looking straight towards the vault. When you reach the springboard, start to push off from the ground with your front foot.

Push off with your front foot.

STEP 2

Whilst pushing off from your front foot, lift your back foot and swing both legs forward with your knees slightly bent to land on the end of the springboard.

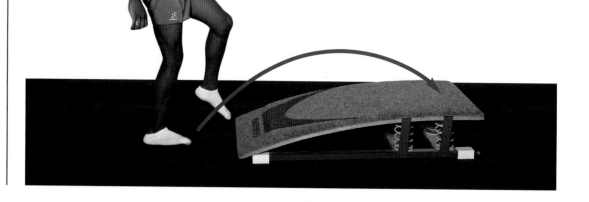

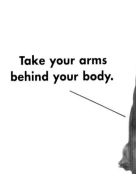

Take your arms behind your body.

STEP 3

Bend your knees slightly when you land on the springboard, and take your arms behind your body. This will lower your chest and assist with the forward drive on to the vault. Push off from the springboard with both feet.

STEP 4

Land on the safety mat in the demi-plié position. Your back should be straight and your hips, knees and ankles should be bent.

Land on the springboard with both feet.

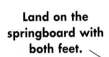

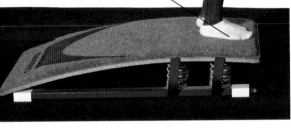

Keep your arms straight.

Keep your knees bent.

Practise doing a handstand against a wall.

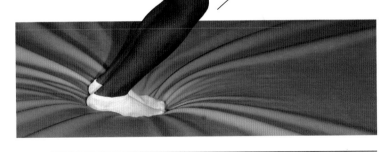

The handstand is a key skill for the vault. Practise doing a handstand on the floor and against a wall.

When you are in your handstand position, shrug your shoulders up and down, this is a good way to learn the technique of 'blocking'. Blocking is when you keep your arms fully extended and straight and push through your shoulders.

TOP TIP

Improve your speed by practising timed sprints up the vault runway.

THE HANDSPRING VAULT

The handspring is a key skill in vaulting. This is an important move for any young gymnast to master. Advanced progressions include somersaults and twisting. The aim is to have a tight body shape throughout the handstand phase and achieve a good flight off the vault. The handspring vault is broken down into five stages.

THE HANDSPRING VAULT

STEP 1
TAKE OFF

Have a strong, fast run up. Your feet should make contact with the springboard in front of your body. Your knees should be slightly bent and your feet should be parallel.

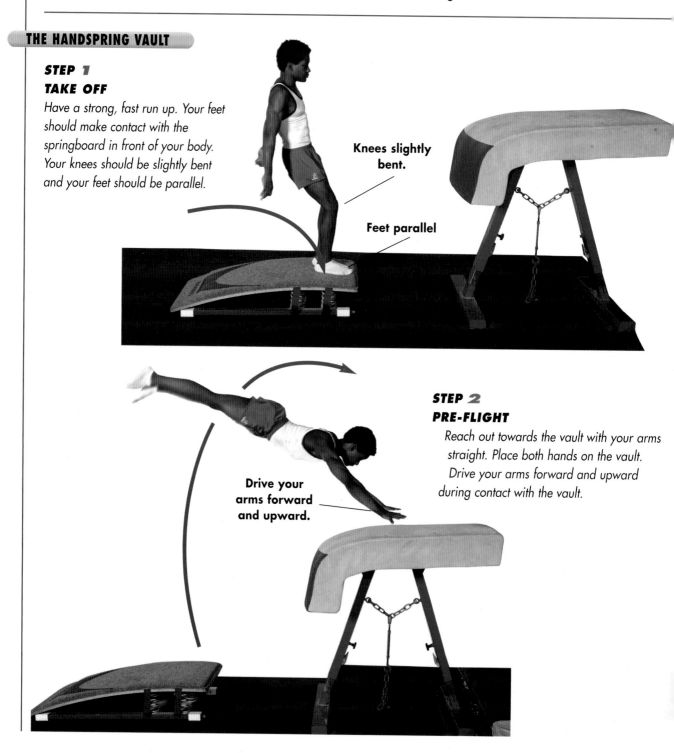

Knees slightly bent.

Feet parallel

STEP 2
PRE-FLIGHT

Reach out towards the vault with your arms straight. Place both hands on the vault. Drive your arms forward and upward during contact with the vault.

Drive your arms forward and upward.

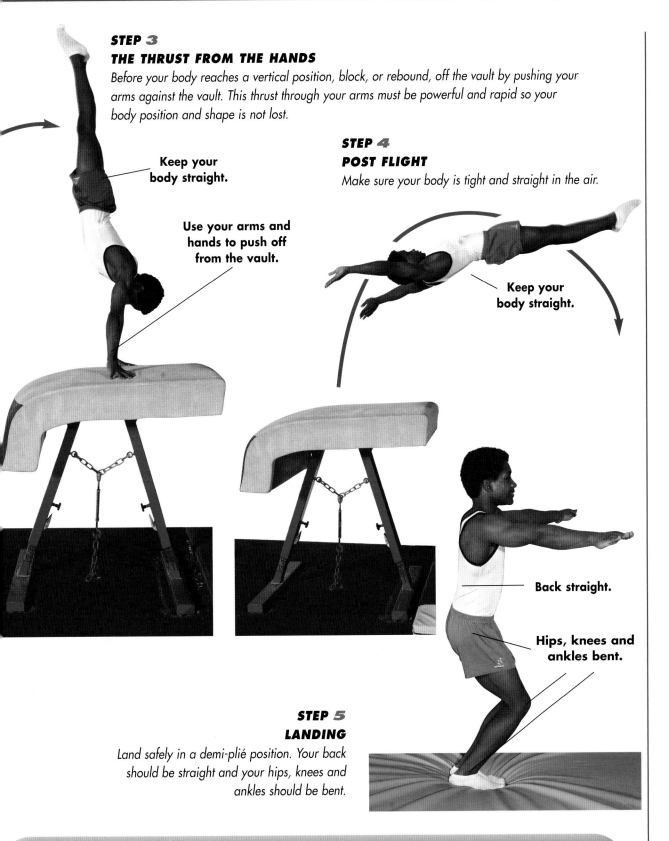

STEP 3
THE THRUST FROM THE HANDS

Before your body reaches a vertical position, block, or rebound, off the vault by pushing your arms against the vault. This thrust through your arms must be powerful and rapid so your body position and shape is not lost.

Keep your body straight.

Use your arms and hands to push off from the vault.

STEP 4
POST FLIGHT

Make sure your body is tight and straight in the air.

Keep your body straight.

Back straight.

Hips, knees and ankles bent.

STEP 5
LANDING

Land safely in a demi-plié position. Your back should be straight and your hips, knees and ankles should be bent.

TOP TIP
The time spent on the springboard should be quick so that you don't lose any speed or power.

FLOOR

Floor routines can be the most spectacular events in gymnatics. On the floor gymnasts can demonstrate impressive acrobatic movements. As women's floor routines are set to music they are particularly popular with audiences and they allow gymnasts to express their personality through dance and musical style.

CHOREOGRAPHY

Choreographers work with top-class gymnasts to compose their floor routines.
They help them create expressive dance movements in-between tumbling passes. On the floor, there are many different styles of routines depending on a gymnast's personality and body shape.

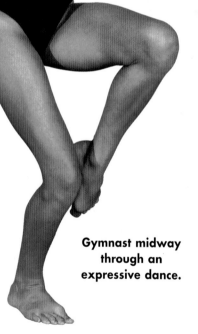

Gymnast midway through an expressive dance.

BALLET

Ballet training from an early age teaches good posture, coordination and spacial awareness.
It also develops poise and grace as it improves strength and flexibility and helps prevent injury. Gymnasts often stand at a ballet barre in front of a mirror. This helps them to correct and improve their technique.

Gymnast at a ballet barre.

Demi-plié

THE HANDSTAND

The handstand is a fundamental move in gymnastics and it is essential to master it in order to progress. It is performed on all pieces of apparatus.

Have a fun competition with your teammates and count how long you can each stay up in a handstand for. The more you practise, the more strength you will build up in your arms and shoulders and the easier it will become to hold it for longer.

STEP 1
Stand up tall with your body fully stretched and your arms straight above your head.

STEP 2
Raise your lead leg and make a deep lunge.

Raise lead leg.

STEP 3
Lean over and take your chest down towards the thigh of your lead leg. The angle between your arms and your chest should remain fully open.

Lunge forward

STEP 4
Place your hands on the floor in front of your lead foot.

STEP 5
Kick into the handstand, this should be a controlled swinging movement of the leg. Your upper body should be in line with your hands. Hold your body tight in a slightly dished shape, with your feet pointed and legs together.

Maintain your balance through your hands and control at your shoulders.

TOP TIP
Practise holding your tight body position in a handstand against a wall.

CARTWHEELS & BACKFLIPS

Cartwheels are one of the most basic skills in gymnastics. Practising and perfecting the cartwheel will develop your upper body and leg strength. By practising the splits, you will be able to achieve a wider straddle in the cartwheel. Always keep your arms and legs straight.

CARTWHEELS

When you have perfected your cartwheel, you can learn more fun skills, such as a one-handed cartwheel, and a round off, which is when you join your two feet together at the end of a cartwheel.

STEP 1

Lift your lead leg to get momentum.

Lift lead leg.

STEP 2

Step forward with a lunge.

Twist your upper body sideways as your chest lowers to floor.

Put your hands down.

Swing rear leg up.

Swing your rear leg up, thrust from your lead leg and put your hands down.

Straddle position.

STEP 3

In the air your legs will pass through the straddle position.

STEP 4

Bring your leading leg downwards and place close to your hand.

Bring leg down close to hand.

Lift your body up by pushing through your hands.

STEP 5

Place your second leg in line with your first leg.

TOP TIP

Practise doing cartwheels one after another in a row and see if you can stay in a straight line.

BACKFLIP

STEP 1
Stand tall with your arms straight up by your ears.

The backflip is one of the most popular moves for an aspiring gymnast to learn as it allows you to travel backwards with speed. Advanced gymnasts who perform tumbling sequences use the backflip as an accelerator, as it makes it possible to go faster backwards and rebound into harder moves, such as back somersaults, twists and layouts.

STEP 2
Bend your knees so that you are nearly in a light sitting position. Lean backwards and keep your heels down. Your knees must remain in line with your toes.

Knees in line with toes.

STEP 3
Rotate backwards with a strong arm swing.

Keep your arms straight.

STEP 4
Remember to keep your legs together and straight.

STEP 5
Spring up quickly from your hands to your feet. As you push through your shoulders, keep your arms straight and your legs will come straight over your head.

Push through with hands and shoulders.

STEP 6
Land with your arms up by your ears. Bend your knees to give yourself a soft landing.

TOP TIP
Always remember that your hands should be parallel in the backflip.

PARALLEL BARS

You need good upper body strength to perform on the parallel bars. You can adjust the width of the parallel bars to suit your height. Usually the width between the bars is set at the same distance as the length between your elbow and the tip of your fingers. A competition routine on the parallel bars consists of swings, flight movements and strength elements. It ends with a dismount off the end or the side of the parallel bars.

STRENGTH HOLDS

To build up the upper body strength required for this piece of apparatus, you must work on strength holds.
These are static movements which you should aim to hold for three seconds, without any adjustments or swinging.

TUCKED HOLD

Tucked hold

Start with your body hanging down in a straight position.
Your arms and shoulders should be locked on the bars to keep you in position. Keep your arms straight. Bend your knees and bring them both gently up to your chest.

Keep arms straight.

LEG LIFTS ON A BOX TOP

Parallettes

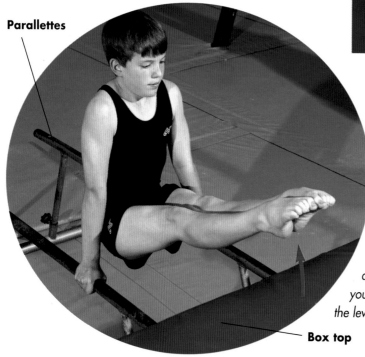

To practise for the lever position on the parallel bars, start on the parallettes by doing lots of leg lifts on a box top.

Paralettes are smaller and lower than parallel bars. Place the box top across them and rest your legs on it. Keep your arms locked to support your weight.

Try going into the lever position holding one leg at a time, leave one leg on top of the box and when you feel ready, raise it up to join the other one to form the lever position.

Box top

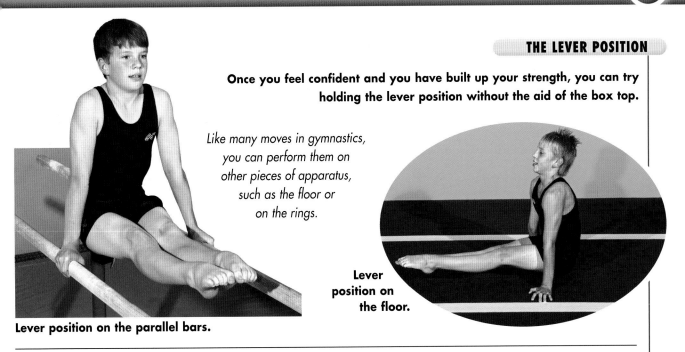

THE LEVER POSITION

Once you feel confident and you have built up your strength, you can try holding the lever position without the aid of the box top.

Like many moves in gymnastics, you can perform them on other pieces of apparatus, such as the floor or on the rings.

Lever position on the floor.

Lever position on the parallel bars.

RUSSIAN LEVER

Lots of body conditioning is required in order to hold a Russian lever.

Once you are in a piked position (with your legs straight and your body bent at the hips), try to bring your legs up towards your face, keeping them straight and controlled. The Russian lever takes many gymnasts a long time to master. To make it easier, try doing the tucked hold, which will mean your legs are bent, and then try and straighten them out and upwards.

Russian lever on the parallel bars.

STRADDLE LEVER

Another good strength hold is the straddle lever.
First you need to sit on the floor in straddle position. Keep your stomach muscles tight and toes pointed, lift yourself up off the ground. To balance, spread your fingers and keep them flat on the floor. Make sure your legs stay straight. When you feel confident, then you can try to perform this lever on the parallel bars with the help of your coach.

Straddle lever on the floor.

THE BASKET SWING

A basket swing is a swing where your shoulders and body are piked and your centre of gravity lies between your shoulders. This is a difficult move because you must learn how to create the swing. By practising this on a rail, it is easier to understand the movement that you need to create on two bars. The amount that you swing is also very short, so it's difficult to gain momentum.

THE BASKET SWING

STEP 1

To get into the position for the basket swing you must go into the inverted pike position. This is where you are hanging upside down with your legs straight and close to your chest.

Hold on to the bars, with your arms straight and your chest facing the ceiling. Kick both legs up so your knees are in front of your face.

Keep your arms and legs straight and start the swing from your shoulders.

Your hands should be on the inside of the bars.

Body in inv[ ]
pike posit[ ]

STEP 2

Keep your head tucked in as you use your shoulders to bring your body forward.

Keep head tucked in.

STEP 3

Lift your shoulders and hips upwards and forwards. Try not to bend. Remember this is a swinging movement, so it is through your shoulders that you will gain the momentum that you need.

Lift shoulders

Lift hips

STEP 4

Keep a tight body position throughout the move. In order to get more swing, pike more at the beginning of the swing as you swing downwards and then open out on the upward phase.

TOP TIP

Practise sitting on the floor in a piked position and lean over with a straight back to lie your tummy flat on to your knees. Keep your knees and arms straight. This will increase the flexibility in your hamstrings.

RINGS: BASIC SWING

*T*he key to a good swinging technique is a well-conditioned body and the ability to maintain a tight body shape throughout the movement. The swing is a key element on the rings, so you should spend a long time practising it.

THE BASIC SWING

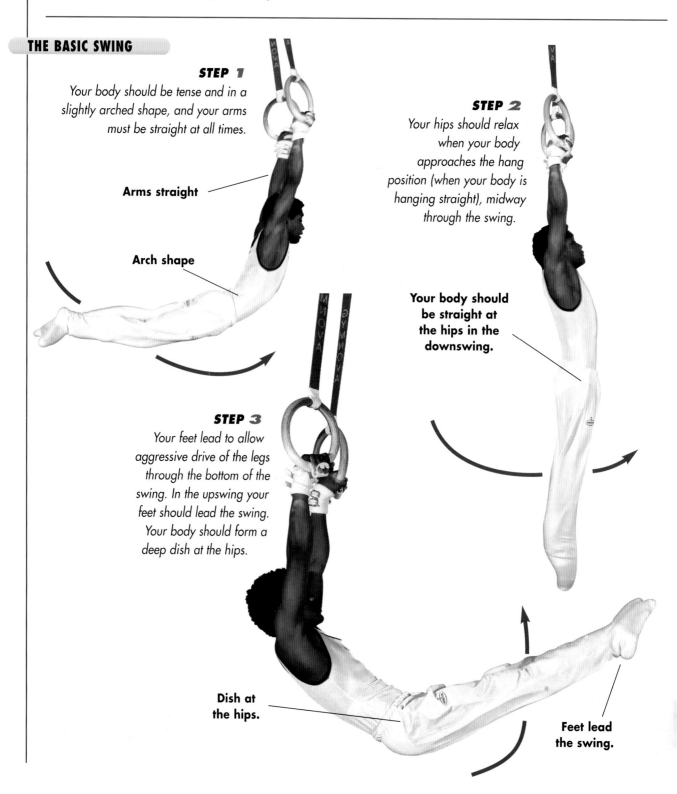

STEP 1
Your body should be tense and in a slightly arched shape, and your arms must be straight at all times.

Arms straight

Arch shape

STEP 2
Your hips should relax when your body approaches the hang position (when your body is hanging straight), midway through the swing.

Your body should be straight at the hips in the downswing.

STEP 3
Your feet lead to allow aggressive drive of the legs through the bottom of the swing. In the upswing your feet should lead the swing. Your body should form a deep dish at the hips.

Dish at the hips.

Feet lead the swing.

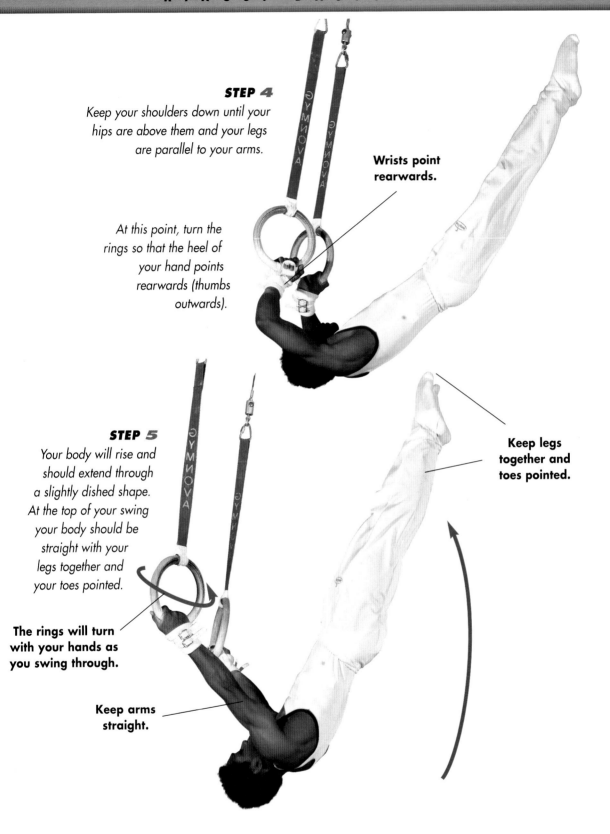

STEP 4

Keep your shoulders down until your hips are above them and your legs are parallel to your arms.

Wrists point rearwards.

At this point, turn the rings so that the heel of your hand points rearwards (thumbs outwards).

Keep legs together and toes pointed.

STEP 5

Your body will rise and should extend through a slightly dished shape. At the top of your swing your body should be straight with your legs together and your toes pointed.

The rings will turn with your hands as you swing through.

Keep arms straight.

TOP TIP

Practise your swinging shape by doing dish rocks. Lie on the floor in a dish shape, with your arms up by your ears and your feet raised. Then gently rock up and down and try to maintain good body tension.

RINGS

*S*winging and strength holds are the main elements of a rings routine. You need good technique in swinging momentum and the ability to hold yourself in a strength hold. This requires tremendous body conditioning.

Tucked hold

STATIC STRENGTH HOLDS

Like on the parallel bars, static strength holds are very important and require practice in order to control and balance the movements.
You can lower the rings closer to the floor, which will make practising your strength holds easier.

TUCKED HOLD

Practise the tucked hold on the rings.
A tuck position is when you have your knees bent and pulled up to your chest. Remember to keep your toes pointed and head looking up, and don't be tempted to swing!

HALF LEVER HOLD ON A BOX TOP

Once you have mastered holding the tuck position you can attempt the half lever hold.
This takes a lot of strength to hold and control. To practise, use a box top, and lift one leg up at a time. This is useful if you find it too difficult to lift both legs up together.

THE HALF LEVER POSITION

Once you feel confident, raise the rings up to the correct height and practise the lever hold in the air.
You might need your coach to help lift you up to the rings.

To perform a series of swings and holds, such as straddle and pike, and then to eventually push up to a handstand on the rings, requires great strength and balance. These drills will improve your balance and control.

Toes pointed towards the ceiling.

Legs straight

INVERTED HANG

The inverted hang will help to develop your balance.
To get into the move kick over into a piked hold – which means your legs will be straight and close to your body. Then push your legs up as high up as you can into a straight body position.

GERMAN OR BACK HANG

To get into the German or back hang position, hold on to the rings with straight arms and bring your legs up into a tucked position.
Then invert yourself, which means hanging upside down. Bring your feet through your hands and over your head and start to straighten them as much as you can and extend through your shoulders.

German or back hang

PIKED INVERTED HANG

Hang upside down, bring your legs straight down together towards your face.
The more supple your hamstrings are, the easier it will be to hang in a pike position.

Piked inverted hang

TOP TIP
Practise holding the half lever by using the support of a box top.
Using this as a platform will help you to balance and to build up strength in your abdominal area.

ASYMMETRIC BARS

The most important skill on the asymmetric bars is the ability to swing. You need a natural fluid swing with good rhythm to perform the high level 'release and catch' moves which are commonplace in elite gymnastics. In competition, your bar routine must be continuous with no stops. The routine must include movement on the low bar and the high bar, movement between them, 'release and catch' elements and a dismount.

TYPES OF GRASP

The most common hand grasps used in gymnastics on the bars are the overgrasp and the undergrasp.

THE OVERGRASP

The hands go under the bar with your palms facing towards you.

THE UNDERGRASP

The hands go over the bar with your palms facing away from you.

BODY CONDITIONING EXERCISES ON THE BARS

Your gymnastics session will include some body conditioning at the end.

Using the bars is an important part of body conditioning routines, as it helps to improve your upper body strength. You should perform all of these exercises slowly and with control. Do not swing into the movements, as this means you are not using all of your body strength.

CHIN UPS

Chin ups will greatly improve your upper body strength.

At first, you may not be able to pull yourself right up to the bar. Your coach can help you with this by holding on to your legs and helping to lift your body weight up so your chin reaches the bar.

Keep your arms straight before you pull up, so you are hanging with a straight body. Bend at the elbows and use your upper arm muscles to pull your chin up to the bar.

Do not swing in to the chin up as you won't be using the right muscles.

LEG LIFTS

Hang on the bar with your arms and legs extended. Raise your legs upwards towards the bar, so your toes touch it.
Your legs should be straight and toes pointed throughout. This exercise will strengthen your stomach muscles, which are called your abdominals.

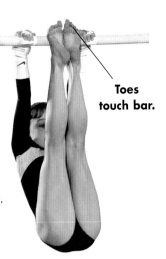

Toes touch bar.

BODY SHAPE

In order to have a good swinging technique on the bars, you must learn the correct body positions that you should be achieving in a swing.
There are two key parts of the swing which you should learn. These are the arch and the dish body shapes.

ARCH

Lie on your tummy and put your arms above your head.
Keep your arms and your legs straight and lift them up off the floor as high as you can.

DISH

Lie on your back and put your arms above your head.
Keep your arms and your legs straight and, as in the arch movement, lift them as high as you can. The higher you go, the more your legs will want to separate, but it is important to keep them together and only go as far as you can in the dish body shape.

PRACTISING BODY SHAPE

Just like on the floor, you can practise holding the same arch and dish shapes while hanging on the bar. When moving between the arch and dish shapes you will pass through a straight hanging position.

Hanging in dish   **Straight position**   **Hanging in arch**

TOP TIP
You can purchase a single bar that will fit onto your door frame at home, so you can practise your conditioning exercises, such as chin ups and leg lifts.

THE FLOAT UPSTART

The float upstart, or 'glide kip' as it is also known, is a very important linking movement on the bars. It is the first move used by many gymnasts to begin their asymmetric bars routine. As a linking move, it allows the gymnast to build up momentum to perform additional, more difficult movements, such as swinging up or casting up to a handstand.

STEP 1

Jump upwards to catch the bar. The trick is to lift your hips as high as you can while still remaining in the pike position. This means your centre of gravity will be high and it will create rotation.

Keep your arms straight.

STEP 2

Float through in a dished shape. End the float with your body straight.

Keep your head in between your arms the whole way through.

STEP 3

Pike at the hips by raising your legs up towards the direction of the bar.

STEP 4

Bring the shins up to the front of the bar. This should be a fast movement so that you don't drop back under the bar.

Drive the bar up the shins and thighs.

STEP 5

As you start to swing back, pull on the bar to drive the bar up your shins and thighs. Coaches sometimes refer to this movement as the trouser pull up, as it is just like this action.

Front support position.

STEP 6

Press down on the bar with straight arms to get your shoulders over the bar until the upstart has finished in the front support position.

Press down on the bar with straight arms.

Body straight and toes pointed.

TOP TIP

You can practise this move at home. Lie on the floor in a pike position holding a broom handle up by your toes. Drive the broom handle up your shins and thighs until your legs are on the floor.

POMMEL HORSE

A typical pommel horse routine involves single and double leg work, known as scissors and circles. Double leg work in the form of circles makes up most of a routine at elite level. This involves the gymnast swinging both legs around the pommels in a circular motion.

LEVELS OF DIFFICULTY

This piece of apparatus is technically very difficult as the gymnast's hands are the only part of his body that are in contact.

Although it requires a lot of strength, technique is probably even more important. To increase the difficulty, a gymnast will add circling and turning movements. Flairs are also commonplace, which is when the gymnast straddles his legs wide and can circle the pommels. In a competition routine, you must include travelling movements and use all parts of the pommel horse. You can practise techniques for the pommel horse on other pieces of equipment before trying the pommel horse.

WALKING ON PARALLEL BARS

You can build up your upper body strength for the pommel horse by doing walks along the parallel bars.

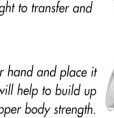

By practising walking up and down the parallel bars, you will get used to holding your weight. Remember to chalk up, so that you do not slip on the bars. Mount the bars from a platform. Push down through your shoulders and be aware not to shrug your shoulders up. By pressing down with straight arms, you will be able to hold your bodyweight up and keep a straight bodyline. Keep your legs straight and toes pointed.

To start walking, you will need to create movement in your body. Lift one hand up and move it along the bar, this allows the bodyweight to transfer and the movement to happen.

Then centre yourself and lift the other hand and place it further along the bar. This exercise will help to build up your upper body strength.

TOP TIP
Do lots of upper body conditioning, as the more strength you build up in this area, the easier it will be to develop your skills on the pommel horse.

To master front support swings on the pommel horse, you must do a series of progressions. *Included here are two for the parallel bars and the rings. When you build up your strength and master the technique, you can then perform them on the pommel horse with greater ease.*

Place your lower arms on the parallel bars or through the rings to support your weight and swing your legs side to side in straddle. Keep your legs straight and extend at the end of the swing.

Use your lower arms to support your weight on the parallel bars.

Legs straight and in straddle position.

Your legs should be straight and extended at the end of each swing.

THE MUSHROOM

Young gymnasts will start learning skills for the pommel horse on the mushroom.

This is a small, rounded piece of equipment which allows gymnasts to perform circle movements easier and for a lot longer than performing on the handles of the pommel horse.

FRONT SUPPORT SWINGS

Having practised the progressions on the parallel bars and on the rings, you should move on to trying them on the pommel horse. When doing front support swings, the legs should remain straddled throughout without closing the straddle at the bottom of the swing. Extend high at the end of your swing.

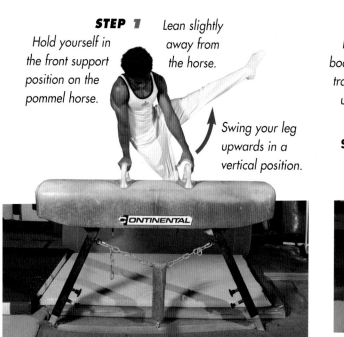

STEP 1

Hold yourself in the front support position on the pommel horse.

Lean slightly away from the horse.

Swing your leg upwards in a vertical position.

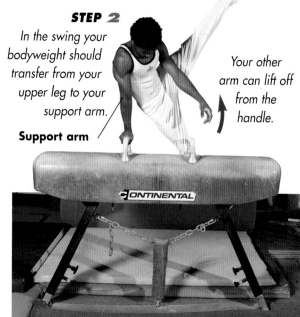

STEP 2

In the swing your bodyweight should transfer from your upper leg to your support arm.

Your other arm can lift off from the handle.

Support arm

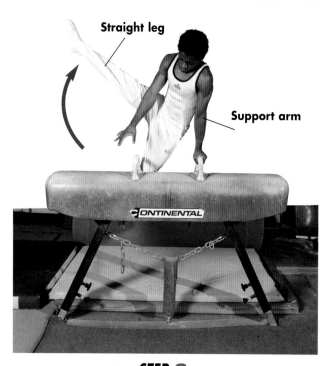

Straight leg

Support arm

STEP 3

The height and form should be equal at both sides of the swing. Your legs should be straight and you should try to achieve height at the end of the swing.

Straight leg

Start to drive lower leg upwards.

STEP 4

As your top leg reaches its peak, you should think about driving the bottom leg upwards. Don't wait until your other leg has come down.

FRONT SHEARS

STEP 1

Start with a front support swing. Your legs should be in straddle position with your right leg high and your left leg at the bottom of the swing.

Take weight on support arm.

The front shears are a progression from the front support swings. It is a diffucult move as you have to swap your legs over to bring one in front of the horse.

STEP 2

Before you replace your right hand on the pommel, swing your right leg down in front of the horse. At the same time drive your left leg up as you would with a front support swing.

Transfer weight so that your other arm becomes the support arm.

Lift arm and swing leg down behind horse.

STEP 3

When your left leg reaches the top of the swing transfer your weight onto your right arm and lift your left arm off the pommel. As you lift your left arm swing your right leg under it.

STEP 4

This is where you swap legs. As your right leg swings under your arm and back behind the horse, drive your left leg down in front of the horse. Replace your left arm on the pommel and get ready to repeat the move on the other side.

TOP TIP
Work on your flexibility. With increased hip flexibility you can achieve more elevation at the top of each swing.

THE BEAM

The beam requires poise and balance. A routine is composed of a mount, acrobatic elements, leaps, turns, dance and a dismount. You should perform with confidence and maintain a good centre of balance so that you don't fall off the apparatus. The top gymnasts on this piece perform with as much ease on the beam as if they were performing the routine on the floor.

FRONT SUPPORT MOUNT

There are various mounts you can perform to get onto the beam.

This gymnast is demonstrating the front support mount. You can jump up to this position by using a springboard. Your head should look up when you reach this front support position. To stand up on the beam, lift one leg over and sit in straddle. Then put your legs behind you and push up on your toes.

You should keep your arms and legs straight and toes pointed.

STAG MOUNT

This is the stag mount, where the gymnast runs up to the beam, bounces onto the springboard and leaps onto the beam, with the leading leg bent at the knee and the back leg straight and extended.

In the stag leap, the front leg is bent and then opened for landing.

WALKING ALONG THE BEAM

It takes time to build up your confidence on the beam. Practise by doing different walks as part of your beam warm-up session.
Keeping a tight body and looking straight forward will help to maintain your balance.

Walk along the beam on your toes with your arms up by your ears.

Walk along the beam lifting one leg up high, with your toes pointed.

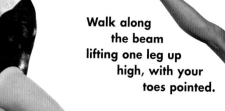

FORWARD ROLL

A good forward roll should be a fluid and smooth movement with no jerkiness.

Practise on the floor, then move to the low beam and gain confidence before doing the move on the high beam. Use a beam mat which will give you some support for your back. Remove the mat when both you and your coach feel confident that you can perform it on the high beam.

STEP 1
Crouch down.

STEP 2
Place the heel of your hands on the beam.

Tuck your head in.

Thumbs should point forwards.

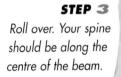

Push off with your feet.

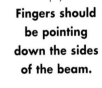

Fingers should be pointing down the sides of the beam.

STEP 3
Roll over. Your spine should be along the centre of the beam.

STEP 4
Continue the roll and put your weight on the landing foot to finish and reach out in front of you.

TOP TIP
Draw a straight line on a mat with chalk to practise your gymnastics moves before moving to the low beam, and then to the high beam.

BACKWARD WALKOVER

There are many moves in gymnastics that involve being upside down. These moves mean that you put all your weight on to your hands. This gymnast is performing a backward walkover.
When you pass through the handstand your legs should be split and straight. Your hands are flat and you will be aware of where to put your standing leg down, so that you does not lose your balance. This movement is also commonly performed going the opposite way, which is called a forward walkover.

FREE FORWARD ROLL

The free forward roll is a more advanced skill, it involves doing a forward roll without using your hands.
To start with you should practise with the beam mat on. Imagine you are rolling your spine along a straight line. Bend your landing leg so it is ready to plant firmly on the beam when you come out of the roll. Then you can stand up.

Hand position is very important. You should always have your hands flat to avoid injuries like broken fingers.

Your arms should be straight and not touching the beam.

Beam mat
This is a soft mat which is placed over the beam to give you added support when practising new moves.

JUMPING

To leave the beam and to jump up into mid air, requires confidence and practice.
At first, you can practise doing low jumps. It is important to practise your landing on the beam. Smaller gymnasts are able to stand on the beam and perform movements, landing with their two ankles beside each other. However, most gymnasts land with one foot in front of the other, with them touching.

Bring your arms behind you, then swing them forwards and upwards so that they are beside your ears.

TUCK JUMP

To do a tuck jump on the beam, bend your knees and bring your arms behind you.
Then swing your arms forwards and upwards (this will achieve height in the jump), and push off from the beam with your feet and knees.

Bend your knees as you jump and bring both knees up towards your chest.

SPLIT LEAP

If you are very flexible you will be able to achieve a good leg extension in your split leap.
Practising your splits while sitting on the floor will increase the range of movement in your hips. Increase your confidence at performing this movement by practising it on the low beam, then move up to the high beam. To achieve height in your leap, push off hard from your leading leg.

TOP TIP
Try not to wave your arms about. Keep them tight and straight as you perform moves. This will help you to balance.

HIGH BAR

Perhaps the most breathtaking piece of apparatus in men's gymnastics is the high bar. Elite gymnasts perform 'giants', which are rotational moves around the bar in the handstand position. This allows the gymnast to build up speed and wind up into big 'release and catch' moves and dismounts with multiple somersaults and twists.

THE CAST

The cast is a move where you swing your legs back and away from the bar up to horizontal position. Maintaining body tension is essential in order to perform a good cast.

The cast on the bar is also known as a 'beat'. Think of yourself as beating away from the bar. A common temptation is for gymnasts to separate their legs at the end of the beat or cast backwards, as they try and achieve more height. Try to imagine that your legs are glued together at all times so that they don't come apart.

STEP 1
Start in front support. Move your shoulders in front of the bar.

Keep your body tight and in a dish position.

Drive your legs backwards.

STEP 2
Swing your legs forwards to get momentum.

STEP 3

Keep your arms straight and your shoulders forward until your hips are above shoulder height.

Beat your legs backwards.

Arms straight

STEP 4

Press forward with your hands on the bar as you raise your legs to open the angle between your body and your shoulders.

Control your swing back down to front support.

Once you have mastered a good cast to front support, the next progression is for your coach to help you in a cast up to handstand on the low bar.

TOP TIP

Tie a pair of socks around your shins so that you can get used to casting backwards with your legs held together.

THE BACKWARD HIP CIRCLE

The backward hip circle is usually performed after the cast. Not only is this move performed on the high bar and asymmetric bars, but it can also be performed on the beam by jumping up to front support and then rotating around the beam.

BACKWARD HIP CIRCLE

This movement involves your whole body circling backwards around the bar.
The move begins when the shoulders begin to lean backwards, which causes the rest of the body to follow. You must keep your hips close to the bar so you rotate the whole way around it. By performing this move after a cast, which means driving your legs backwards and upwards and then returning back to the bar, it gives you momentum so that you can go straight into the backward hip circle, and you will rotate around the bar.

STEP 1
Start in front support.

Press down on the bar and move shoulders backwards.

STEP 2
Use your legs to lead the swing down around the bar. Keep your body in a tight dish shape.

Keep your body tight, with your arms and legs straight, and your legs together.

Your feet will lead the swing around the bar.

Rotate wrists

Regrasp bar

Press bar on to thighs

STEP 3
You must stay close to the bar in the rotation by pressing the bar on to your thighs.

STEP 4
Continue rotating around the bar and finish in the front support position by pushing up onto your straight arms.

TOP TIP
Remember to chalk up and wear handguards so that you have a better grip on the bar.

COMPETITION

The biggest event in the gymnastics calendar is the Olympic Games, which is held every four years.
The World Championships are the qualifying event for the Games. All gymnasts compete in a qualification round, through which they can qualify for the team final, the all-around final and the individual apparatus final. Other major competitions in the gymnastics calendar include the European Championships and the Commonwealth Games.

Daiane dos Santos of Brazil performs on the floor in the World Championships.

NATIONAL SQUADS

To compete at international level requires years of training and competing. Gymnasts work their way up by doing grades and competing at regional level.
A select few are then chosen for the junior national squad before moving up to the senior squad when they are old enough. At national squad level, gymnasts will perform in many competitions so that they get used to competing in front of an audience and learn how to cope with nerves and pressure.

FIG

The governing body for gymnastics is the Federation Internationale de Gymnastique (FIG).
The FIG produces the rulebook of gymnastics known as the 'Code of Points'. This document is updated and revised at the end of every Olympic cycle. It sets out the difficulty value of each element in routines and what the requirements are for each piece of apparatus.

In 1997, the FIG introduced an age limit for international competitions.

The minimum age to compete is 16 years old. Having an age limit means that younger gymnasts do not compete at a level that is too high and experience too much stress. It also gives older gymnasts the chance to keep competing.

The most significant change in the 'Code of Points' has been the abolition of the perfect '10'.

Gymnastics now uses open-ended scoring. There are two panels of judges, one who judge the difficulty of the routine, the other panel judge the execution (how well it is performed).

Judges view a performance of a gymnast on the pommel horse.

A *value = 0.1 points*	
B *value = 0.2 points*	
C *value = 0.3 points*	
D *value = 0.4 points*	
E *value = 0.5 points*	
F *value = 0.6 points*	
G *value = 0.7 points*	

There are specific elements that a gymnast must perform in their routine and these requirements will vary depending on the level of competition.

Elements are graded from A to G, with A being the easiest and G the hardest.

DIET

A gymnast needs fuel to be able to train and a balanced diet will ensure you are getting all the necessary vitamins and minerals. A balanced diet should combine carbohydrates, fat, protein and fibre.

This diagram shows the percentage of foodstuff that should be eaten to maintain a balanced diet.

Drink liquids little and often. Avoid sugary drinks as they provide no nutrient value, are loaded with calories and are gas-forming.

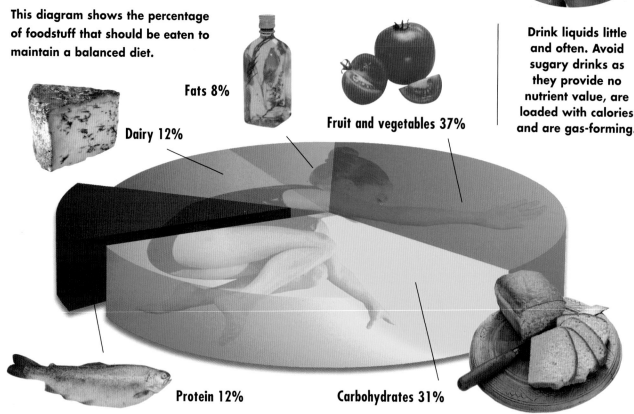

Fats 8%

Dairy 12%

Fruit and vegetables 37%

Protein 12%

Carbohydrates 31%

CARBOHYDRATES, FATS AND PROTEINS

Carbohydrates, fats and proteins are the nutrients which provide energy.

Foods like pasta, rice, potatoes, bread and cereal contain carbohydrates. They release the energy required for dynamic training and explosive energy immediately. Fats and proteins supply energy over a longer period of training. Protein is found in animal products, such as meat, poultry, fish and dairy foods. Having fresh fruit and vegetables in your daily diet will provide you with vitamins and minerals.

THE CALORIE COUNT

Elite gymnasts keep a watchful eye on their calorie intake in order to control their weight.

All food that we eat contains a number of calories. Foods which are high in fat contain more calories and will require more exercise to burn off. Active gymnasts will burn around 3,000 to 3,500 calories per day, so they must eat this amount of calories in order for their weight to remain the same.

TOP TIP

Eat about one and a half hours before a training session. This gives enough time for the food to be properly digested. Eating a snack one and a half hours after training is also advisable.

MENTAL ATTITUDE

*G*etting to the top in gymnastics requires long hours of training and also a strong mental focus. It requires a lot of time away from friends and family, as gymnasts must travel to competitions and training camps. Rest is also very important, as it allows both body and mind to recover after a work-out.

THE COACH

A gymnastics coach should always encourage a gymnast and take them through the correct progressions in order for them to advance in a manner that is right for them.
The safety and welfare of gymnasts should always be of the highest importance. Goal-setting will motivate gymnasts to train to develop skills and work towards performing them in competition. Sometimes, a gymnast experiences disappointment. This can be difficult to deal with and requires positive thinking, and lots of support from their coach. After competing, the coach and gymnast sit down and talk about the competition, set out goals for the next competition and adapt the training programme if necessary.

Gymnast and coach in discussion – getting in to the zone.

Gymnasts need good concentration to perform at the highest level.

CONCENTRATION

A high level of concentration is required in training and when competing.
It is important to perform safely and stay focused as this will minimise the risk of injury. Psychologists help gymnasts to focus their mind using different strategies. Thinking positive thoughts, such as "I can do this," creates a positive mental attitude. Gymnasts are also trained to visualise what they want to achieve. Whether it's mastering a certain move or winning the gold medal in a competition, a positive focus is a powerful influence.

HOW THE FAMOUS DO IT

*A*lthough gymnastics has been around for more than 2,000 years, it has been a competitive sport for little more than 100 years. During this time, the sport of gymnastics has changed immensely and routines have become more and more spectacular.

DEVELOPING ELEMENTS

Up until the 1960s, gymnastics remained mostly a male sport, dominated by gymnasts who were renowned for their strength.

The top nations at the time were Japan and the Soviet Union. The difficulty of skills being performed was always being increased, new elements were being introduced and gymnasts who were the first to perform them had those elements named after them. Alexander Tkatchev performed a high level 'release and catch' move on the bar in 1976, and the Tkatchev is still being performed today.

WOMEN SUPERSTARS

Olga Korbut (Belarus)

Traditionally women gymnasts performed with grace and their movements were slow and controlled, a style which was made famous by Soviet gymnast Ludmilla Tourischeva, who won the all-around gold at the 1972 Olympic Games.

In the 1970s some truly remarkable gymnasts caused a sensation that would change women's gymnastics forever. With her elfin physique and big personality, Soviet gymnast Olga Korbut won the hearts of millions at the 1972 Olympic Games in Munich. Korbut turned women's gymnastics into the popular sport it is now and inspired a whole new generation of children to do gymnastics. Standing only 149 cm tall, the 17 year old performed spectacularly difficult routines. Her back somersault on the beam was regarded as a daring move and her floor exercise sparkled. She became known as the 'Munchkin of Munich', the darling of the Olympics.

Also credited for popularising the sport is Nadia Comaneci, a 14-year-old Romanian who, under the guidance of her coach Bela Karolyi, set a new standard in gymnastics – that of perfection.
Her performance on the asymmetric bars at the 1976 Montreal Olympics earned her the first-ever perfect '10' in the history of the sport. She went on to score six more perfect '10's and win three gold medals at these Olympics.

CURRENT OLYMPIC ALL-AROUND CHAMPIONS (BEIJING, 2008)

The powerhouse nations such as the USA, Russia and China continue to produce superstars in the sport. Their daredevil performances and high-level skills amaze audiences around the world.

Nastia Liukin (USA)
Anastasia Liukin, or Nastia as she is known, won the Olympic all-around final at the 2008 Olympic Games in Beijing. Liukin is the only child of two former Soviet champions, Valeri Liukin and Anna Kotchneva. The family moved to America when Nastia was 2 years old and now live in Texas. Nastia is admired in the gymnastics world for her grace and elegant long lines.

Yang Wei (CHINA)
Chinese gymnast Yang Wei is best known for his impressive ability on all six pieces of apparatus. He won the all-around title at the 2008 Olympic Games in Beijing.

WHAT HAPPENS NEXT?

After a career competing in gymnastics, many gymnasts often go into coaching, or study to become a judge.
Some take up scholarships with colleges where they can continue to train while furthering their education. Other gymnasts who have achieved world success turn professional, which means they are paid for all their commercial appearances.

GLOSSARY

ABDOMINALS – *Also known as 'abs', these are the stomach muscles.*

ALL-AROUND – *Competition format in which the gymnast competes on every piece of apparatus.*

APPARATUS – *The equipment male and female gymnasts perform and compete on.*

ARCH – *When the body is in arch position the back is curved back and the arms and legs are stretched back.*

BALLET BARRE – *A bar made of metal or wood, which gymnasts hold on to and practise ballet moves on. The barre can be freestanding or mounted on a wall.*

BICEPS – *The muscles in the upper arms.*

BLOCKING – *Keeping your arms fully extended and straight and pushing through your shoulders.*

CHOREOGRAPHER – *A professional who creates dance routines.*

CODE OF POINTS – *The rule book of gymnastics.*

CONDITIONING – *A physical preparation programme to improve strength.*

DEMI-PLIÉ – *A ballet position which involves bending your knees while keeping your heels on the floor.*

DISH – *When the body is in dish position the back is curved forward and the arms and legs are forward.*

HAMSTRINGS – *The muscles at the back of your thighs.*

PIKE – *A position where the body is bent at the hips and legs are straight and raised towards the trunk of the body, forming a 'L' shape.*

PIROUETTES – *Turning while standing on one leg.*

POISE – *Performing a movement with grace and elegance.*

PSYCHOLOGIST – *Expert in dealing with the way the mind works.*

SPLITS – *A position where the legs are extended in opposite directions either one in front of you and one behind, or out to the sides.*

STRADDLE – *A position where the legs are open wide and extended in front of the body.*

TRAVELLING – *Moving along an apparatus while performing on it.*

TUCK – *The legs are bent and raised towards the trunk of the body.*

WARM UP – *Exercises performed at the beginning of a training session to get the body and muscles warm.*

LISTINGS

European Union of Gymnastics (UEG)
*Avenue de Rhodanie 2
PO Box 188
1000 Lausanne 6
Switzerland
Tel: 0041 21 613 7332
Fax: 0041 21 613 7331
www.ueg-gymnastics.com*

Federation Internationale de Gymnastique (FIG)
*Avenue de la Gare 12
1003 Lausanne
Switzerland
Tel: 0041 21 321 5510
Fax: 0041 21 3215519
www.fig-gymnastics.com*

British Gymnastics Association
*Ford Hall
Lilleshall NSC
Newport, Shropshire
TF10 9NB, UK
Tel: 0845 129 7129
Fax: 0845 124 9089
www.british-gymnastics.org*

USA Gymnastics
*132 E. Washington St.
Suite 700
Indianapolis
IN 46204, USA
Tel: 001 317 237 5050
Fax: 001 317 237 5069
Member Services: 1 800 345 4719
www.usa-gymnastics.org*

Gymnastics Australia
*32 Cleeland Road
Oakleigh South, VIC
3167
Australia
Tel: 0061 03 9271 0500
Fax: 0061 03 9271 0599
www.gymnastics.org.au*